IMAGES
of Sport

BRISTOL ROVERS
FOOTBALL CLUB

IMAGES
of Sport

BRISTOL ROVERS
FOOTBALL CLUB

Compiled by
Mike Jay

TEMPUS

First published 1999, reprinted 2000, 2003

Tempus Publishing Limited
The Mill, Brimscombe Port,
Stroud, Gloucestershire, GL5 2QG

British Library Cataloguing in Publication Data.
A catalogue record for this book is available from the British Library.

ISBN 0 7524 1150 0

typesetting and origination by Tempus Publishing Limited
printed in great britain by Midway Colour Print, Wiltshire

Contents

Foreword

It is a great honour to be asked to write a foreword for this wonderful book, which depicts a pictorial history of Bristol Rovers Football Club.

I am a third generation Rovers supporter and I have, of course, ensured that the fourth generation is in place to continue my family's tradition! However, it is sometimes difficult to describe to others the great teams, players and events of the years gone by.

Memories of my first visit to Eastville on Boxing Day 1964, to watch a thrilling 3-1 victory over Queens Park Rangers in front of a partisan 17,000 crowd, are flooding back to me as I write: the anticipation as the car was parked in an Eastville side street and the excitement of the crowd queuing for the turnstiles at the Tote End of the ground. The smell of tobacco smoke mixed with the pungent odour from the nearby gasworks produced an intoxicating cocktail as The Pirates ran out onto the muddy Eastville pitch...Heaven!

How can we convey to our more junior supporters an insight into the past of our unique club? Mike Jay has found a way, by producing this superb book of photographs which will bring back memories for some of you and give the less fortunate a glimpse of the 'Good Old Days'!

We can trace the club's early history – as far back as the Black Arabs and Eastville Rovers and the Southern League days and election to the Football League in 1920. This was followed by the financial problems of the 1930s, which ended in the club seeking re-election and selling the freehold of Eastville Stadium to the Greyhound Company in 1940. The successful team of the early 1950s, under the guidance of Bert Tann, reached the sixth round of the FA Cup in 1951, before being beaten by the mighty Newcastle United in a replay. The Division Three (South) championship was won two years later. The promotion years of 1974 (with Don Megson at the helm) and 1990 (under Gerry Francis), as well as the Wembly appearances in 1990 and 1995, all provided moments to cherish.

Bearing in mind that the club has endured two major grandstand fires at Eastville and Twerton Park and that, as a result, many records and pictures have been destroyed, Mike Jay must be congratulated for painstakingly putting together this compilation, which constitutes a unique pictorial history of Bristol Rovers Football Club.

Thank you once again Mike, for your dedication in providing another superb publication on Bristol's oldest football club.

Geoff Dunford
Vice Chairman Bristol Rovers FC
February 1999

Introduction

Supporting Bristol Rovers over the past thirty years has seen many highs and lows. Besides the highs of promotion and lows of relegation, the cultural move from Eastville to Twerton Park, Bath, in 1986 was a major disappointment. Many sceptics saw it as possibly the end of Bristol Rovers FC. However, the move triggered a new impetus as 'Ragbag Rovers', as they were described by the media, developed into a formidable unit under the guidance and astute management of Gerry Francis. Promotion and Rover's first ever trip to Wembley in the Daf Cup Final in 1990 was achieved and these remain personal highlights for myself and, I should imagine, all fans of the club.

Financially, Rovers have never been able to compete with the big clubs in the transfer market, so they have had to produce their own players. There have been many notable examples of Rovers players who have had to be sold and have gone on to play at the highest level: Cliff Britton, Ronnie Dix, Phil Taylor, Larry Lloyd, Gary Mabbutt and Nigel Martyn have all represented England and played in the top flight.

Many believe the sale of Eastville Stadium in 1940 to the Greyhound Company for £12,000 was a major turning point in the club's history. However, it was not until 1986 that the financial situation reached crisis point. Wide-ranging management changes had to be implemented and there were major cuts in the budget for both staff and players. This was due to a struggling team on the pitch with ever-decreasing numbers of supporters. Of course the impact of extensive television football coverage only served to make matters worse. During those dark days, a succession of players have had to be sold to ensure the club's continued existence, notably Nigel Martyn, Gary Penrice, Marcus Stewart, Gareth Taylor, Marcus Browning and, most recently, Barry Hayles.

One of the most disappointing and unresolved problems over the past two decades has been a lack of co-operation by Bristol City Council to positively assist Rovers in finding a suitable site to develop a new, all-seater stadium. The move to sharing the Memorial Ground and to eventually own the stadium has fulfilled a dream of many generations of Rovers supporters – a home of their own back in Bristol. Rovers directors Denis and Geoff Dunford have steadfastly worked, against all odds at times, for a new, purpose-built stadium and I believe they should now be publicly acknowledged as the saviours of the club. Without their positive dedication, particularly in the late 1980s, much of the entertainment and enjoyment provided by numerous Rovers teams since that time would not have been appreciated by generations of supporters. In short, the club would probably have gone out of business without the intervention of the Dunfords.

Compiling this book has underlined to me what it feels like to support a club through the good and bad times. While Rovers have never reached the top division, we can at least hold on to the fact that they have also never played in the basement division. The demolition of Eastville Stadium in October 1997 was an emotional experience for many older Rovers supporters as years of history have now been physically removed by the bulldozers. I will certainly always remember my favourite matches at Eastville: particularly my favourite Rovers player of all time – winger Harold Jarman, who used his skill and speed to take on an opponent before hitting a powerful shot past the goalkeeper to receive the acclaim of the supporters in the North Enclosure.

My thanks are extended to Rover's official photographer, Alan Marshall, who has taken many thousands of photographs of the club and events over the past twenty-five years. Many of his photographs are included in these pages. Others who have kindly contributed images are Bert Hoyle, Keith Brookman, Ernie Clark, Alan Casse, Geoff Dunford, John Kelland and Alan Williams. Some other pictures have come from the *Bristol Evening Post*, *Bath Evening Chronicle* and the *Bristol Times and Mirror*.

Thanks to my family – wife, Sue, and children, Kelly and Ian – for their encouragement to help me to complete this book. My children are a new generation of Gasheads, who have been encouraged to support their local club. I sincerely hope we will all see the Rovers in the Premiership one day.

I hope you enjoy the book as much as I enjoyed putting it together.

Mike Jay
February 1999

Home, sweet home – Bristol Rovers became owners of the Memorial Stadium in July 1998.

One
The Early Years
Southern League Football

Eastville Rovers, 1894. This is the Rovers team pictured before their first Gloucestershire Cup final, against Bristol St George, on 31 March 1894. The team was, from left to right, standing: W. Stone, C. Hodgson, F. Lovett, H. McBain, L. John. Seated: E. Furze, W. Taylor, A. Laurie, Bob Horsey. On ground: W. Rogers and S. Attwell. St George won the cup 3-1.

Eastville Rovers, 1897/98 season. This was when the club became a limited company and, remarkably, were one of five professional clubs in Bristol at the time: Bedminster, Clifton, South End and Warmley were the others. From left to right, back row: Pay, Horsey, Farnell, Turley, Kinsey, Bunch, Roach. Middle row: Shenton, Draycott. Front row: Cotterill, Jones, Green, Glitheroe, McLean.

EASTVILLE ROVERS FOOTBALL CLUB, LIMITED.

INCOME ACCOUNT
From 5th April, 1897 to 31st May, 1898.

To Players Wages			1051	1	3	By Season Tickets &c	88	7	1
" Commission and Bonus			127	10	.			
" Match Expenses						" Gate Money and Sundry Receipts	1914	15	9
Tea Money, Hotel Expenses								
Railway Fares	170	6	9					
Players' Outfit	45	5	9			" Sundries	40	.	2
Referees	11	19	2					
Gatemen & Checkers	1	12	9			" Balance to Balance Sheet	1237	14	2
Entrance Fees	45	7	6	274	11	11		
" Gate Money paid away			499	1	6			
Printing, Advertising, postage & Sundries			144	11	7			
Formation of Ground including Wages, hauling, Horse Hire, Materials, Stands, Hoarding &c.			958	14	.			
Law Expenses			37	14	6			
Rent & Taxes			114	17	9			
Players Insurance			25	5	-			
Balance taken over from Old Club			47	1	4			
Bankers Charges			3	8	2			
			£3280	17	2		£3280	17	-

Edwin J. Richards
Chartered Accountant
Bristol 1st July 1898

The Eastville Rovers balance sheet from 1898 shows that £958 was spent on forming the ground at Eastville and £1,051 on players' wages, whilst £1,914 was received from gate money.

The club changed its name to Bristol Rovers for the 1898/99 season. John McLean became the club's first professional. From left to right, back row: Pay, Farnell, Bunch, Cook, Griffiths, Turley, Kinsey. Middle row: McLean, Jones, McCairns, Smellie, Fisher. Front row: Brown, Paul.

"BRISTOL ROVERS" FOOTBALL GROUND, EASTVILLE.

This is a rare sketch of Eastville, taken from a weekly publication, *The Magpie* newspaper, of 27 April 1899. In the background it shows the thirteen arches and also a small grandstand.

The Black Swan Hotel, Stapleton Road, Eastville, was Rovers' headquarters and the club offices from 1897 until 1910.

The South Stand at Eastville, c. 1905. It had just 100 seats and was replaced in 1922 with a larger grandstand, which incorporated the dressing rooms, press box and club offices.

Bristol Rovers' ground, 1905. The picture is taken from the *Book of Football*.

Rovers were Southern League Champions for the first and only time in the 1904/05 season. Their regular team is pictured here, from left to right, back row (playing staff and coaches only): Ben Appleby, Tom Tait, Hugh Dunn, Arthur Cartlidge, Dick Pudan, Gavin Jarvie. Front row: George Pay (Trainer), Billy Clark, Jack Lewis, Billy Beats (Captain), Andrew Smith, Arthur Dunkley and Alf Homer (Secretary/manager).

Left: George Humphreys, chairman of Bristol Rovers. He was a very supportive gentleman, who had a great deal of involvement in shaping Rovers' future. *Right:* Alfred Homer, Rovers' secretary from 1899 until 1920. He was effectively the club's first manager. Homer's experience, with Aston Villa, was useful when signing new players for Rovers.

Left: Arthur Cartlidge, Rovers' long-serving goalkeeper, who was with the club from 1901 until 1909. Stoke-born Cartlidge was six feet tall and weighed fourteen stone. He made 258 Southern League appearances for Rovers, then moved to Aston Villa, where he won a League Championship medal, before returning to Stoke in 1911. *Right:* Billy Beats was Rovers' centre forward from 1903 until 1906. Beats went on to win two England caps with Wolverhampton Wanderers. An experienced marksman, Beats proved to be a popular player. He scored forty-four goals in ninety-four Southern League appearances in his three seasons with the club.

Rovers finished in sixth position in the Southern League in the 1907/08 season. The top goalscorer was John Roberts, with fourteen goals in twenty-nine matches. Their squad was, from left to right, back row: Cox, Hales, Sweet, Appleby, Cartlidge, Phillips, Gerrish. Middle row: Murphy, G. Pay (Trainer), Clark, Shapcott, Smart, Strang, Handley, Boyle, Buckle. Front row: Savage, Turner, Smith, Roberts.

Top goalscorer in the 1913/14 season was Ellis Crompton, who netted thirteen times for Rovers. The squad was, from left to right, back row: Brown, Harvie, Roney, Stansfield, Bennett. Middle row: Roe, Nevin, Walker, Westwood, Morris, Brogan. Front row: Peplow, Dixon, Crompton, Murray, Kay, Squires, Griffiths.

Bristol Rovers' Football Club, Ltd.

HARRY ROE'S BENEFIT MATCH.

Lady Munitioners (Brislington Beauties)
v.
H.M.S. "Colossus" XI. (Beatty's Boys)

For date of Match see Posters.

Tickets, 6d. each.
The charge for this Ticket does NOT INCLUDE the Amusement Tax.

Mr. H. ROE, who broke his ankle on Bristol City Ground, November 17th, has a wife and five children to support.

This is a ticket for Harry Roe's benefit match. Rovers have always had a good reputation for looking after their players. The game was arranged because Roe had broken his ankle and the match receipts were used to support his family.

BRISTOL ROVERS FOOTBALL CLUB, Limited.

Ground: Stapleton Road, Eastville.
Telephone No. 51.

Secretary: A. G. HOMER,
Bristol Rovers' Ground, Stapleton Road, Bristol.

DATE AS POSTMARK.

Dear Sir,

Please be down on Saturday. Kick off 3·30 p.m. Even if you do not play for us I shall arrange for you to play for Swindon. Kind regard

Yours sincerely,
A. G. Homer

Postcard from 1918, advising Arthur Baker, a Rovers player, of his selection for a match. Players did not have telephones in those days, so this was the usual way in which they were contacted.

Rovers continued during the First
World War, frequently playing a series
of friendly matches against RAF or
Army units based in the West Country.
The team from the 1917/18 season
included Arthur Baker.

Gyles Bros., Ltd
THE Football Outfitters of the West
500 DOZ. JERSEYS to select from

ANY DESIGN MADE TO ORDER.

SEND FOR PRICE LIST.

OUTFITTERS BY APPOINTMENT TO

GLOUCESTERSHIRE F.A.	BRISTOL AND DISTRICT.
SOMERSET COUNTY F.A.	BRISTOL AND SUBURBAN.
HAMPSHIRE F.A.	BRISTOL DOWNS LEAGUE.
DORSET COUNTY F.A.	BRISTOL WEDNESDAY.
BRISTOL ROVERS A.F.C.	BRISTOL CHURCH OF
WESTERN LEAGUE	ENGLAND.

BRISTOL SCHOOLS LEAGUE. &c., &c., &c.

24, BRIDGE STREET,
and
188, WHITELADIES ROAD,

'PHONE NO. 2888

Bristol.

Gyles were suppliers of strip for Bristol
Rovers and this is their advertisement
from a 1918 football annual.

Programme for Millwall v. Rovers, 24 January, 1920. It was both clubs' last season in the Southern League. They played each other in their inaugural Division Three (South) match just eight months later.

Team line-ups from the Millwall programme.

Two

Into the Football League

The 1920s

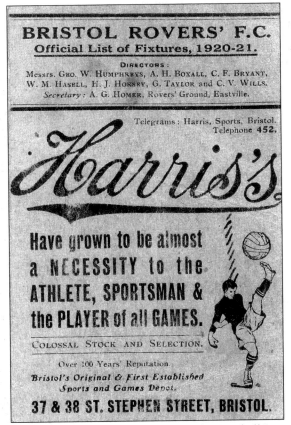

A fixture card for the 1920/21 season – Rovers' first in the Football League Division Three (South). Forthcoming opponents included Swindon, Norwich and Portsmouth.

BRISTOL ROVERS'

Official Programme.

| No. 4. | SATURDAY, SEPT. 25th, 1920. | 2d. |

• • • The • • •

SPORTS NEWS

— IS —

BRISTOL'S BEST.

Never miss — Saturday Night's

SPORTING PINK

*It always contains Full Reports of the Rovers'
Matches, whether home or away, and the
latest news from the Rovers' Training Camp.*

RACING EDITION

Every morning at 10 a.m.   The smartest in the West.

This was the programme for the third home match of Rovers' first season in the Football League, played against Brighton & Hove Albion on 25 September 1920. Rovers won the game 3-1.

'Gentleman' Jesse Whatley, Rovers' popular goalkeeper, was rewarded with a benefit match against Portsmouth, which raised £500, in 1925. Whatley retired in 1930, having completed 372 League appearances.

Rovers' squad included a young winger called Joe Walter, who was sold to Huddersfield at the end of the 1921/22 season. Walter won a League Championship medal with The Terriers, under the management of Herbert Chapman, in 1923. Pictured here, from left to right, are: Joe Walter, Jerry Morgan, Bill Payne, Steve Sims, Jimmy Kissock, Jesse Whatley, Sid Leigh, Jack Ball, Billy Palmer, Tom Winspear, David Steele.

21

Wally Hammond played as a winger for Rovers in the 1922/23 season. He later became a Gloucestershire and (world-renowned) England international cricketer. From left to right, back row: Taylor, Liddell, Boxley, Leigh, Woodward, Whatley, O'Neill, Boyce, Armitage, Parker. Middle row (seated): Furness, Currie, Sambridge, Smith, Lunn, Haydon, Hammond. Front row (on ground): Chance, Morgan, Rose, Wainwright, Lea.

GETTING READY FOR THE KICK-OFF!
Both With the Same "Goal" Ahead.
—Drawn by Mr. F. G. LEWIN, R.W.A.

A *Sports Times* cartoon from 15 August 1925. The rivalry between both Bristol clubs was really established after the very first League derby in 1922, a game held at Ashton Gate and which Rovers won 1-0.

THE BRISTOL EVENING NEWS, MONDAY, MARCH 5, 1928.

A Newsy Page for Sportsmen

Ronald Dix (white shirt), the 15-year-old ex-schoolboy International, playing for the Rovers. Shoots for goal, but Illman (Norwich) saves after the full-back had missed the ball.

Ronnie Dix, at 15 years and 180 days, became the youngest-ever goalscorer in the Football League when he scored against Norwich City at Eastville on 3 March 1928. This is a record that still stands today.

The Re-election Shark hovers around Bristol Rovers' shaky craft, casting its gloating optics on "Eastville Jane". Let's hope it steers off and finds other prey, far away from the Froom Banks.

Re-election cartoon from the *Sports Times* during the end of the 1927/28 season. Rovers struggled for three seasons, finishing nineteenth, nineteenth and twentieth, but only actually had to apply for re-election on one occasion, during the 1938/39 season.

Popular goalkeeper Jesse Whatley had a cartoon commemorating his 200th consecutive appearance. He did, in fact, complete 246 matches before injury curtailed this fine record (which included not missing a single match in five seasons).

Three
The First Quarters
The 1930s

The 1931/32 season was the first one in which the blue-and-white-quartered shirts were adopted by the club. It was argued that the players looked physically bigger in quarters! From left to right, back row: Williams (Assistant Trainer), Storer, Routledge, Calvert, Berry, Stoddart, Oakton, Lake (Trainer). Middle row: Findlay, Hill, Cooper, Hudson, Bryant, Carter, Townrow, Smart, Riley. Front row: Russell, Bennett, Dix, Attwood, Menzies (Assistant Secretary), Captain Prince Cox (Secretary/manager), Pickering, Young, Black, Muir.

Ronnie Dix, a very talented forward, scored two brilliant goals for Rovers against Holland on 16 November 1930. Dix was sold for £3,000 to Division One Blackburn Rovers in 1932. He later enjoyed spells with Aston Villa, Derby County and Tottenham. He won an England cap in 1938.

Arthur Attwood contributed Rovers' third goal in the fine 3-2 victory over the full Dutch international team in the friendly match in Amsterdam.

BRISTOL ROVERS IN
Sun. **HOLLAND.**
16·11·30
SURPRISED BY DUTCH TEAM BUT JUST WIN.

GREAT RIGHT WINGER.
By Valcan.

Holland .... 2 Bristol Rovers... 3

AMSTERDAM, Sunday.

BRISTOL ROVERS had something of a shock playing against a Dutch eleven here to-day, and were perhaps lucky to win.

This must be said for the Rovers, however. They had a hard game on Saturday and crossed the North Sea immediately afterwards. If the players had five hours' sleep they did better than I.

Yet, allowing for these facts, the Rovers did not realise the change that has come over Continental football. They wanted to hold the ball and do tricks and by so doing they played into the hands of the speedy Dutchmen. Time and again the Englishmen were fiddling for position, only to discover that the ball had gone.

I have seen much football on this side, but to-day it has improved out of all knowledge. One gets the impression that Continental football is mechanical, as though taught in stages. But if you give the players time to start their machine they take some stopping. Frankly, the Rovers were often beaten by tactics that are described in our text-books, but are so rarely seen in English football.

One instance was the pass from outside-right to inside-right and the return pass to the winger that travelled inside the on-coming defender. Many times the Bristol left-wing defenders were floundered and hopelessly lost by this simple move.

This Holland team, by the way, have a great right winger. The speed and trickery of Gerritse were amazing. Holland, too, seem to discover goalkeepers. It is many years since I saw so many brilliant saves in one game. Keiser has some rivals in his own country.

The Rovers owed their victory to two brilliant goals by Dix, that wonderful boy footballer who was discovered by the Bristol club. Attwood got the other goal. Both the Dutch points came from breakaway and were scored by their centre-forward. One, however, was yards offside.

The Rovers should do better in their next game at The Hague on Tuesday, which, by the way, will be played under artificial light, but they must play the English open game.

Holland XI.: Odijk; Diepenbeek, Wanders; Entjes, Pap, Breitner; Gerritse, Ruisch, Huisman, De Brock, Van Nelles.

Bristol. Berry; Barton, Richardson; Black, Dinsdale, Hamilton; Forbes, Ball, Attwood, Dix, Young.

Match report of Rovers' friendly in Holland. Two days later they also played and beat Swallows 4-2 under floodlights.

Vivian Gibbins, a London schoolteacher, in action against Brentford on 17 December 1932. Earlier in the season he made press headlines when the club chartered an aeroplane so that he could play in a mid-week match. He landed at Whitchurch airport and the trip proved successful, as he scored against Southend in Rovers' 3-1 victory. Gibbins netted fifteen goals in thirty-seven matches.

Transport for away matches was always undertaken by railway. Chairman George Humphreys (centre) very often paid for these trips from his own money, as the club were financially struggling to survive.

Rovers in France, 1932. Rovers' long-serving trainer, Bert Williams, is on the far left of the picture. Williams spent over fifty years working for the club. He was rewarded with a testimonial against Sheffield Wednesday in 1962.

Rovers coming out to play Milan at the San Siro, May 1933. Milan won the game 3-1. Manager Prince Cox had numerous contacts in Europe, following his earlier days as a distinguished referee.

Rovers and Nice teams pictured prior to their friendly match in France, May 1934.

The Rovers team that played against Nice was, from left to right, back row: Donald, Preddy, Routledge, Lewis, Watson, McLean. Front row: Pickering, Eyres, Smith, Gollop, Wallington.

In the 1934/35 season, Rovers finished sixth in Division Three (South) and won the Division Three (South) Cup, defeating Watford 3-2 in the final, which was played at Millwall. Rovers' squad for that season was, from left to right, back row: Pickering, Ellis, Smith (Jack). Middle row: McNestry, Havelock, Wallington, McLean, Murray, Donald. Front row: Captain Prince Cox (Secretary/manager), Hope, Wipfler, McKay, Smith (Jim), Prout.

Bristol Rovers in the 1935/36 season. From left to right, back row: Robertson, Ellis. Third row: Williams (Trainer), Taylor P., Harris, Frater, Young, Murray, Lake (Trainer). Second row: Barley, Harwood, Rose, Hill, Preece, Wildsmith, Woodman, Adcock, Crisp. Front row: McArthur, McCambridge, McLean, Captain Prince Cox (Secretary/manager), Hawkins (Assistant Secretary), Pickering, Donald, Taylor A., Wallington.

SCORES 10 GOALS!

Luton Gamble That Came Off

13 · 4 · 36

PAYNE BREAKS RECORD IN DEBUT AS LEADER

By FRANK POXON

Luton 12   Bristol Rovers 0

THERE was football drama in excelsis at Luton yesterday.

The position was this. Luton, at the top of the Southern Section, were fighting desperately to keep that position, and they knew they were up against strong opposition teams who were fighting as hard as themselves to gain the status of the Second Division.

Should there be a " gamble "? That was the question.

There was a conference of directors and one bold spirit said: " Why not play Payne at centre-forward on Easter Monday against Bristol Rovers ? "

THE PLUNGE TAKEN

There was a gasp of astonishment and then two or three directors said: " Why not ?

Yes, why not ? True, Payne was a reserve and a half-back at that, but—well, why not ? The plunge was taken and Joe Payne was played yesterday as leader of the attack. He did moderately well—I am sure you will agree !—for he scored ten goals ! And Payne had never before played centre-forward for Luton's first team.

What a debut ! It was a debut unprecedented in the long history of Soccer, for a man making his first appearance at centre-forward in a League side to score ten goals.

A MODEST HERO

He was very modest about it all after the match. He said to me: " It would be silly on my part to say that it was all luck, for I do believe I played well. I am a very happy fellow today. But please give your praise to Stephenson, who ' made ' nearly all our goals."

That was a just comment, for Stephenson was indeed the " universal provider."

He is sturdy, he is fast and he plays for his side and not for himself. To me, yesterday, he looked an international all over. He is a real team man and quite unselfish.

But what an odd thing that Luton have been " entertaining an angel unawares " in Payne. For myself, I just can't understand it. If Payne is not a first-class centre-forward, I am no judge at all. True, many chances were made for him, but he was always " there."

TALE OF THE GOALS

Luton scored two very good goals in the first half-hour. Payne got the first with a shot which gave Ellis no chance, and Roberts got the second. The prelude to this second goal was a shot from Stephenson, which Ellis parried but could not clear.

The third goal was similar to the second in that Stephenson's shot led up to it ; in this case it was Payne who put on the finishing touch. Two or three minutes later Payne got the fourth goal and completed his hat-trick.

The match was well won and lost at half-time, but just to make sure Payne completed a sequence of seven goals in a row and Martin completed the scoring.

A TEAM INSPIRED

Martin once bundled Ellis and the ball into the net, a perfectly good goal from a fair charge, but the referee held that Payne had scored before the charge.

Luton were now playing like a team inspired and Payne could do no wrong. He was living his " moment "—and how he lived it !

Payne is a native of Bolsover. I think he may be a " native " of England's XI. before long. He is a real centre-forward with tremendous dash and a sure shot in each foot. He stands 5ft. 11in. and weighs 12st. Yes, and when a chance comes along his brain is packed in ice.

Luton: Dolman; Mackey, Smith; Finlayson, Nelson Godfrey, Rich, Martin, Payne, Roberts, Stephenson.

Rovers: Ellis; Pickering, Preece; Wallington, Murray, Young; Barley, Hartill, Harris, Houghton, Crisp.

Match report for Rovers' record 12-0 League defeat at Luton Town on 13 April 1936. It was a personal milestone for Town forward Joe Payne, as he scored ten of the goals – a record which has never been matched.

Rovers 1 Arsenal 5, 11 January 1936. Rovers' goal was scored by Harold Houghton in this exciting FA Cup third round tie held at Eastville.

Bristol Rovers, 1936/37 season. From left to right, back row: Raven, O'Mahoney, Pickering, Nicholls, Preece, Harris, Moyle (Trainer), Watson. Front row: Bruce, Mills, Woodman, Houghton, Tidman, McLean.

Above: A ticket for the Arsenal match. The club was heavily criticised for increasing admission prices for the tie, a decision which restricted the gate to just over 24,000.

Right: Matt O'Mahoney, Rovers' Irish international centre half, who won a club record seven caps between 1938 and 1939.

The manager, Captain Albert Prince Cox, left, after six seasons, in October 1936. The players presented him with a carriage clock for his time spent at the club. He left Rovers to promote professional wrestling and boxing in the Plymouth area.

Albert Butterworth scores Rovers' winner at Torquay in a 2-1 victory on 18 March 1939. This was one of just ten wins during the season, which ended with Rovers bottom of Division Three (South) for the only time in their history. They successfully applied for re-election (with forty-five votes), leaving Gillingham unsuccessful (with fifteen).

No. 1. AUGUST 26, 1939.   N⁰ 679   Price : Twopence.

BRISTOL ROVERS FOOTBALL CLUB, Lᵀᴰ
OFFICIAL PROGRAMME.

ALWAYS OPEN
DAY & NIGHT
(24 HOURS SERVICE)

Phone : 64013 (Day and Night).
Telegrams: "Morservice, Bristol."

ASHTON GATE REPAIR WORKS — BY DAY

BRISTOL MOTOR CO. LTD

HEAD OFFICE: ASHTON GATE, BRISTOL, 3

REPAIRS WHILE YOU SLEEP.
A boon to everybody who owns
a Car or Commercial Vehicle.

MAIN AGENTS—
Morris Cars.
Morris Commercial Vehicles.
Sunbeam.   Talbot
OTHER AGENCIES—
Wolseley. Lanchester Daimler

ASHTON GATE REPAIR WORKS — BY NIGHT

This was the programme for Rovers' last League match before the Second World War, against Reading, on 26 August 1939. The war halted professional League football for six seasons. With debts of £20,000, the club sold the ground, on 3 March 1940, to the Greyhound Company, for £12,000.

Many of Rovers' players were called up for the Services and most of them returned to play whenever possible. This is a team photograph from the 1945/46 season. From left to right, back row: Needs, H. Smith, Davis, Gardiner, Allen, Baldie, Long, Jennings, Topping, Butterworth, Mann (Instructor). Middle row: Bissicks (Director), Giles, Meacham, Watkins, O'Brien, Weare, Studley, Frowde, Bridge, Williams (Trainer), Cooper (Trainer). Front row: Champney (Director), Parkinson, Bamford, Peacock, W. Smith, Ferrari (Secretary), Warren, Fletcher (Manager), Lambden, Morgan, Petherbridge, Whitfield, Hare (Vice-chairman).

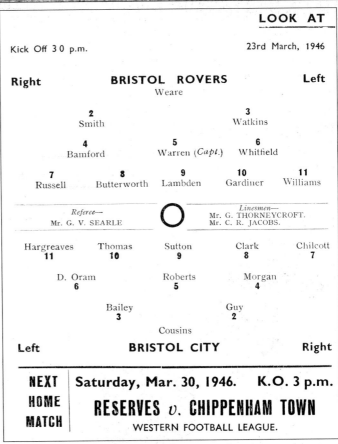

LOOK AT

Kick Off 3 0 p.m.   23rd March, 1946

Right   **BRISTOL ROVERS**   **Left**
Weare

2   3
Smith   Watkins

4   5   6
Bamford   Warren (*Capt.*)   Whitfield

7   8   9   10   11
Russell   Butterworth Lambden   Gardiner   Williams

Referee—   ◯   *Linesmen—*
Mr. G. V. SEARLE   Mr. G. THORNEYCROFT.
                           Mr. C. R. JACOBS.

Hargreaves   Thomas   Sutton   Clark   Chilcott
    11   10   9   8   7

    D. Oram   Roberts   Morgan
       6   5   4

         Bailey   Guy
           3   2

              Cousins

Left   **BRISTOL CITY**   **Right**

NEXT HOME MATCH	Saturday, Mar. 30, 1946. K.O. 3 p.m.
	RESERVES *v.* **CHIPPENHAM TOWN**
	WESTERN FOOTBALL LEAGUE.

Rovers *v.* Bristol City programme, 23 March 1946. With the paper shortage at this time, programmes consisted of single sheets. This Third Division (South) Cup match ended 0-0.

Loyal Rovers full-back Harry Bamford was a talented and popular Bristol-born footballer who, in thirteen seasons, made 486 League appearances (a tally which has only ever been beaten by one player).

Rovers' long-serving captain, Ray Warren, had a well-deserved benefit match against Cardiff City in 1947. The gate was 30,417 and Rovers won 1-0, thanks to a goal from Lance Carr.

Football returns after the
Second World War, in the
1946/47 season. Manager
Brough Fletcher and captain
Ray Warren herald the new
season.

Bristol Rovers 1946/47
season. From left to right,
back row (players only): Jack
Pitt, Jack Weare, Harry
Bamford, Wally McArthur,
Ray Warren, Barry Watkins.
Front row: Ken Wookey, Len
Hodges, Fred Leamon, Jimmy
Morgan, Lance Carr.

Bristol Rovers, 1947/48 season. From left to right, back row: Pitt, Warren, Weare, Bamford, Watkins, McArthur. Front row: Wookey, Hodges, Lambden, Morgan, Petherbridge.

OFFICIAL RACE CARD   SIXPENCE

EASTVILLE - 94th Meeting

UNDER THE RULES OF AND LICENSED BY THE NATIONAL GREYHOUND RACING CLUB).

WEDNESDAY EVENING, NOVEMBER 9th, 1949

1st RACE (737) 7.30 p.m.   Winner £5 2nd £2 3rd £1   500 Yds

1 Red — TANERA — E. RODGERS—Banister.
bd.d. Marvellous Rush—Living Fury. June, 1946.

2 Blue — BUSH FLOWER — S. P. BARTLEY—Banister.
f.b. Barkaway—Crubany Bush. January, 1948.

3 White — COMBE DOWN — A. J. STILL—Mercer.
bd.d. Marvellous Rush—Living Fury. June, 1946.

4 Black — RIVER MODEL (W) — R. E. BABER—Mercer.
bd.w.d. Dancing Model—Castlewood Blonde. Mar.,47.

5 Orange — KETCHY (W) — F. J. CHALKE & L. J. HOOPER.—Mercer.
bd.d. Thady The Thief—Parmatta. January, 1947.

6 Stripes — MADEMOISELLE FIFI (W) — P. A. HUGHES & C. R. HUGHES—Parker.
bd.b. Keel Radio—Wild Hilarity. February, 1947.

APRIL 18th, 1949, IN SEASON.

Greyhound racing card for a meeting at Eastville. Racing took place at the stadium from 1928 until 27 October 1997.

Four
Promotion At Last
1953 – The First
Championship

Bill Roost prepares to challenge the Ipswich Town goalkeeper in the game on 22 August 1949.
Roost scored twice in this match, which Rovers won 2-0.

George Petherbridge was a diminutive winger who made 452 League appearances for Rovers between 1946 and 1962, in which time he scored eighty-five goals. Petherbridge scored fourteen in the 1951/52 season, which included four against Torquay United.

Jack Pitt was a hardworking and skilful half-back, who completed 467 League appearances for Rovers between 1946 and 1958. He had a spell as coach at the club and was the groundsman at Eastville and Twerton Park for over thirty years.

Cartoon of the Rovers *v.* Millwall Division Three (South) match of 11 March 1950. Drawings such as these were a popular feature during this era, this one was by 'Pak'.

BOARD OF TRADE

COMPANIES ACT 1948

Inspection of Bristol Rovers Football Club Limited

REPORTS OF
A. FRANK WARD, F.C.A.

Published pursuant to Act 11 & 12 Geo. 6. c. 38, s. 168

LONDON: HIS MAJESTY'S STATIONERY OFFICE
1951
PRICE 2s. 6d. NET

The 1951 Board of Trade inquiry into the affairs of Rovers and the Greyhound Company found many irregularities and resulted in both companies being separated.

Rovers goalkeeper Bert Hoyle is well covered by his defence – Harry Bamford (2) Geoff Fox (3) and Jack Pitt (4) – during the FA Cup tie against Hull City on 10 February 1951.

Action from the FA Cup sixth round tie at Newcastle United, which attracted over 63,000 fans, on 24 February 1951. Over 5,000 Rovers supporters made the long journey to the North East and were rewarded with a replay after a goal-less draw. In this shot, United's Jack Milburn is being closely watched by Geoff Fox.

There were 31,000 tickets available for the Newcastle FA Cup replay and over 100,000 people brought Stapleton Road to a standstill for many hours as they queued for them on 26 February 1951.

In the replay, played on 28 February 1951, Rovers went ahead through Geoff Bradford but, unfortunately, Rovers full-back Geoff Fox (above) scored an own goal for Newcastle's equaliser. United won 3-1 and went on to win the FA Cup.

Rovers' squad pictured during a training run, *c.* 1951. Much of the daily training involved long runs to develop stamina. Surprisingly, not much time was spent training using the football.

Goodnight Irene, the popular song, was adopted by Rovers supporters throughout their eleven-match FA Cup run. It is still sung by each new generation of supporters at almost every game.

Eastville under water, 1951. This was a regular occurrence throughout this period. The pitch was raised by four inches to try to stop flooding from the River Frome, which ran alongside the South Stand. Flood-relief work was completed in 1968 and this finally resolved the problem.

Rovers' goal comes under pressure from Preston in a third round FA Cup tie on 12 January 1952. Bamford, Petherbridge, Pitt and goalkeeper Hoyle are the players pictured. Rovers won the match 2-0.

OFF BRADFORD'S HAT-TRICK.—No. 1, Bradford taps the ball into the net shortly after the t. (2) Newport's defenders watch Bradford's header (from Pitt's free-kick) sail over their ds into the open goal—the scorer and the goalkeeper are lying on the ground. (3) Acting goalkeeper Birch makes a vain attempt to stop the header from Petherbridge's centre.

Newspaper photographs of the three goals which ensured promotion to Division Two on 25 April 1953, following the 3-1 defeat of Newport County at Eastville.

Supporters celebrate the club's first promotion with a pitch invasion after the final whistle against Newport.

Left: Manager Bert Tann became the Football League's longest-serving manager, having guided the Rovers from 1949 until 1967. Tann's major achievement was winning the Division Three (South) championship and establishing the club in Division Two throughout the 1950s. He remained with the club as general manager until his death in 1972. *Right:* Ron Moules was the club secretary. He was with Rovers from 1949 until his death in 1967. Ron was a true blue, who harangued the local press if the club received less coverage than their nearest rivals.

The Rovers championship squad of the 1952/53 season scored a club record ninety-two goals and were widely recognised as an entertaining football side with many gifted individual players who worked hard for each other. From left to right, back row: Jack Pitt, Harry Bamford, Bert Williams (Trainer), Geoff Fox, Vic Lambden. Middle row (players only): Bert Hoyle, Peter Sampson, Howard Radford. Front row (players only): Bryan Bush, John McIlvenny, George Petherbridge, Ray Warren, Geoff Bradford, Bill Roost, Josser Watling.

The autographs of the 1952/53 team.

Rovers supporters, including Mrs Bradford, pictured at Whitchurch Airport before the trip to watch Geoff Bradford play for England in Denmark on 2 October 1955.

Geoff Bradford scoring in the England match, which was a 5-1 victory. Unluckily, Bradford did not add to his solitary cap.

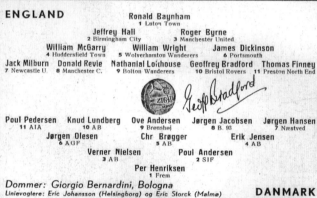

ENGLAND

Ronald Baynham
1 Luton Town

Jeffrey Hall   Roger Byrne
2 Birmingham City   3 Manchester United

William McGarry   William Wright   James Dickinson
4 Huddersfield Town   5 Wolverhampton Wanderers   6 Portsmouth

Jack Milburn   Donald Revie   Nathanial Lofthouse   Geoffrey Bradford   Thomas Finney
7 Newcastle U.   8 Manchester C.   9 Bolton Wanderers   10 Bristol Rovers   11 Preston North End

Poul Pedersen   Knud Lundberg   Ove Andersen   Jørgen Jacobsen   Jørgen Hansen
11 AIA   10 AB   9 Brønshøj   8 B. 93   7 Næstved

Jørgen Olesen   Chr Brøgger   Erik Jensen
6 AGF   5 AB   4 AB

Verner Nielsen   Poul Andersen
3 AB   2 SIF

Per Henriksen
1 Frem

Dommer: Giorgio Bernardini, Bologna
Linievogtere: Eric Johansson (Helsingborg) og Eric Storck (Malmø)

DANMARK

Programme for the Denmark v. England match. Bradford was joined in the forward line with the established stars Jack Milburn, Don Revie, Nat Lofthouse and Tom Finney.

Geoff Bradford wearing his England cap. It was an honour which established him as the only Bristol Rovers player ever to win a full England cap while with the club. If he had not suffered two serious injuries, it is probable his international career would have been extended.

BRISTOL ROVERS OVERWHELM MANCHESTER UNITED

Bristol Rovers 4, Manchester United 0

Bristol Rovers, playing irresistible football, swept Manchester United from the Cup scene with scant respect for reputations. If this, to the world at large, was one of the surprise results of the third round there was certainly no question about its execution to those at Eastville on Saturday—for Bristol Rovers, if their present mood is sustained, are clearly destined for further success.

Manchester United, except for brief periods in the opening half, were never in the match, for they made the fatal mistake of employing tactics unsuitable to the cloying conditions. In consequence their delicately linked game was made to look ponderous in the mud by opponents quick in anticipation and resolute in the tackle.

By contrast, Bristol Rovers favoured an open approach, combined with a precision and an enthusiasm which, in themselves, were an object lesson, and with every man rising to the occasion there was only one logical result. The real surprise, in fact, was to be that Manchester United, finding themselves two goals in arrears at half-time, still persisted in their tactics and thereafter faded more and more from the scene leaving Bristol Rovers to hold the stage at the final curtain.

OPENING THRUST

After the usual preface of cup-tie histrionics, somewhat subdued in this instance, Manchester United supplied the opening thrust in the fifth minute when Taylor ran on to a forward pass from Doherty to test Nicholls from an angle. Bristol Rovers, however, were soon seen to advantage in attack and although Pegg and Berry again worried their defence with a wing to wing move to give Viollet a chance with his head, they retaliated sharply in the tenth minute with an opening goal. It was Meyer who initiated the movement with a long cross-field pass which Petherbridge used to effect by cutting inside Byrne and centring for Bradford to challenge Jones in the air; the ball ran loose to the edge of the penalty area and Biggs gave Wood little chance with a great drive.

This was indeed an encouraging start for the underdog and Bristol Rovers might have gone farther ahead ten minutes later when Biggs met a deep cross to the far post, again from Meyer, only to head straight into Wood's arms. But Manchester United, meanwhile, had not been idle in attack and one particularly promising move was only scotched when Bamford obstructed Pegg just outside the penalty area. From the resulting free kick Byrne pierced the defensive screen with a drive just inside the post, but the referee had clearly indicated an indirect free kick and the Mancunian celebration was short-lived.

Four minutes later, however, they nearly did equalize when a fierce shot by Taylor was deflected across the face of the goal by Nicholls; but it was not to be, for seconds before half-time Bristol Rovers went further ahead with a similar move to their opening goal. This time, it was Bradford who supplied Petherbridge with the pass to cut inside Byrne and there was Meyer to meet the short centre and recover from an air shot to beat Wood from close range.

COMPLETE CONTROL

Soon after the resumption Manchester United made great efforts to narrow the gap but, after Nicholls had saved a flying header by Taylor and a neat chip shot from Pegg, Bristol Rovers took complete control of the game by scoring their third goal in the sixtieth minute. There was an element of luck attached to the incident, however, for Biggs was clearly in an offside position before he went on to beat Wood, and the only supposition can be that Byrne had unwittingly played him onside as he went in to tackle Petherbridge, who had supplied the final pass. Be that as it may, from then onwards Manchester were subjected to a series of sharp raids each one of which emphasized Bristol's undoubted superiority. First Biggs forced a corner with a great drive, then Bradford was only inches wide with a header from Hooper, who had suddenly materialized on the right wing. Another header by Biggs from Hooper, now on the left, again forced a corner and then Hooper himself took a hand with a terrific drive which Wood did well to save.

And so it went on until finally, six minutes from the end, Byrne in desperation handled to save his lines to give Bradford a well deserved goal from the penalty spot and complete a memorable victory. Teams:—.

BRISTOL ROVERS.—Nicholls; Bamford, Allcock; Pitt (captain), Hale, Sampson; Petherbridge, Biggs, Bradford, Meyer, Hooper.
MANCHESTER UNITED.—Wood; Foulkes, Byrne (captain); Colman, Jones, Whitefoot; Berry, Doherty, Taylor, Viollet, Pegg.

Rovers' finest result was on 9 January 1956, when they beat the mighty 'Busby Babes' 4-0 in the third round of the FA Cup. This is the match report from *The Times*.

Rovers' first goal, scored by Alfie Biggs (out of the photograph), against Manchester United. He later added a second, along with further goals from Barrie Meyer and Geoff Bradford.

Goalkeeper Ron Nicholls, who was a Gloucestershire cricketer during the summer, pulls off a tremendous save to deny United's England centre forward Tommy Taylor.

Season ticket book for 1955/56, which was one of the finest seasons in the club's history, Rovers finishing sixth in Division Two.

Left: Bristol Rovers' Supporters' Club membership card. The club had a membership of over 17,000 during this era and raised many thousands of pounds for Rovers. *Right:* Inside the Eastville dressing rooms just prior to kick off, *c.* 1956. Harry Bamford, George Petherbridge and Ian Muir prepare for action.

54

Team spirit – one of the strengths of the club was the tremendous friendships of all the staff and players. Here, Geoff Bradford and Harry Bamford share a joke.

Dai Ward was a talented footballer, but at times a controversial figure with Rovers' manager, Bert Tann. He once scored a hat-trick, against Doncaster, in just four minutes. Ward won a Welsh cap in 1958 against England. He scored a total of ninety goals in 175 League appearances for Rovers, before his transfer to Cardiff City in 1961.

Peter Hooper was a gifted left-winger who, whilst with Rovers, represented the Football League against the Irish League in 1960. Hooper had so much power in his shots that goalkeepers were often weary about playing against him.

Leeds United's John Charles heads the winning goal against Rovers at Elland Road in a 2-1 defeat on 21 April 1956, which ended Rovers aspirations for promotion to Division One.

Geoff Bradford played for Rovers from 1949 until 1964. He became the club's record goalscorer, with 242 goals in 461 League appearances. Besides his one England cap, he represented the FA in a tour of the West Indies. His Rovers career included nine League hat-tricks. Bradford bravely fought back twice from serious injury to become Rovers' most famous player.

Alfie Biggs played for Rovers from 1953 until 1961 and again from 1962 until 1968. A popular Rovers forward, nicknamed 'The Baron' by his team mates, Bristol-born Alfie enjoyed two spells with Rovers and spent eighteen months at Preston. He scored 178 goals in 424 League appearances. His thirty-three goals in the 1963/64 season remains a club record.

Dai Ward scores the first of his two goals against West Ham United at Eastville on 31 August 1957. However, The Hammers triumphed 3-2.

Barrie Meyer played for Rovers from 1950 until 1958. He was a talented forward who managed sixty goals in 139 appearances. Barrie went onto become a noted professional cricketer and, for many years, was a famous and well-respected international umpire.

Norman Sykes scores against Notts County in a 3-0 victory at Eastville on 9 February 1957.

Bristol Rovers, 1957/58 season. From left to right, back row: Edwards, Sampson, Sykes, Radford, Hale, Bamford, Doyle. Front row: Watling, Petherbridge, Biggs, Bradford, Ward, Meyer, Hooper, Pitt.

A Bob Bennett cartoon illustrating Rovers' 7-0 home defeat by Grimsby Town on 12 October 1957.

Action from the Bristol derby at Ashton Gate on 14 December 1957. David Pyle is beaten in the air by City's John Atyeo (9), watched by Rovers players Petherbridge, Ward and Sampson.

Friendly banter as the Pirates' mascot meets the Robins' mascot before the exciting fifth round FA Cup tie at Ashton Gate on 15 February 1958.

Bristol City goalkeeper Bob Anderson dives bravely at the feet of Rovers forwards Barrie Meyer and Dai Ward in the cup tie.

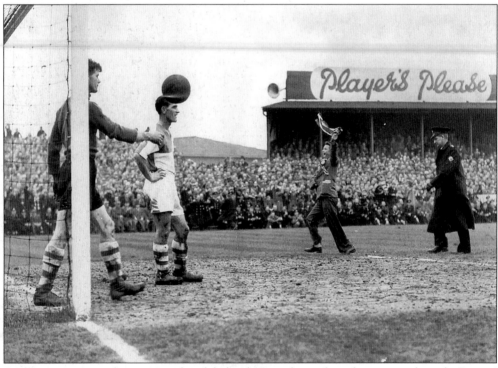

An impromptu pitch invasion by delighted City fans after their second goal. Rovers' goalkeeper, Ron Nicholls, and defender, Josser Watling, are not amused.

Geoff Bradford scores Rovers' fourth and what proved to be the winning goal. It was controversial and many City supporters years afterwards said it was offside! Rovers won the game 4-3.

The *Pink 'Un* sports paper's headline heralds a fine FA Cup victory.

Rovers supporters prepare for their train journey to Fulham for the sixth round FA Cup tie on 1 March 1958.

Geoff Bradford scores Rovers' consolation goal at Craven Cottage in a match which Fulham won 3-1.

Rovers and Fulham supporters happily mix during the cup-tie.

Rovers supporters at the Tote End of Eastville Stadium, c. 1958.

Peter Hooper scores a cracking goal against Liverpool in a 3-1 victory at Eastville, March 1958.

Dai Ward scores Rovers' first goal against Fulham, in a Division Two match which ended 2-2, 4 April 1958.

Rovers finished in sixth position in the 1958/59 season and Dai Ward scored a remarkable twenty-six goals in thirty-seven League appearances. From left to right, back row: Norman Sykes, Peter Sampson, David Pyle, Howard Radford, John Watling, Brian Doyle. Front row: George Petherbridge, Alfie Biggs, Geoff Bradford, Dai Ward, Peter Hooper.

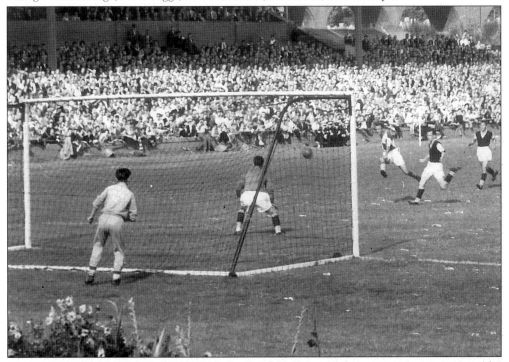

Rovers' new North Grandstand was opened for the first time on 30 August 1958. The Supporters' Club paid a substantial amount towards the building costs. This photograph shows Geoff Bradford shooting on the Scunthorpe goal.

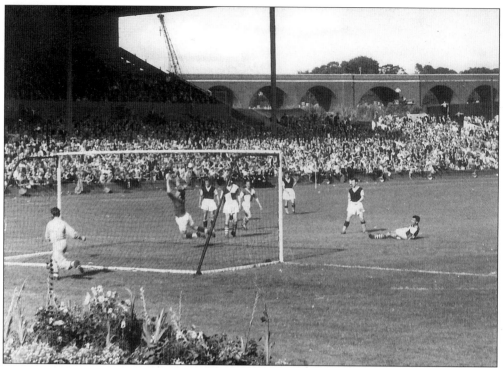

Goalmouth action as Rovers attack the Tote End during the Scunthorpe match. Note the roses behind the goal, which were a feature of Eastville for many years.

Rovers and City teams line up, on 1 November 1958, for a minute's silence to pay their respects, following the death of Harry Bamford in a motorcycle accident.

In the ensuing match, Dai Ward prepares to shoulder charge Bristol City goalkeeper Tony Cook. The visitors won the game 2-1.

Dai Ward scored twice in this remarkable match, on 15 November 1958, when Rovers beat Grimsby Town 7-3. Peter Hooper scored a hat-trick and Geoff Bradford netted twice in the game.

**THE HARRY BAMFORD
MEMORIAL MATCH**

COMBINED BRISTOL XI
v.
ARSENAL

FRIDAY, 8th MAY, 1959

Kick-off 6.45 p.m.

SOUTH STAND 5/-
"B" Block

Row **K**   Seat No.   **53**

THIS PORTION TO BE RETAINED.

IN THE EVENT OF POSTPONEMENT, TICKETS AVAILABLE ON
RE-ARRANGED DATE; NO MONEY REFUNDED.

Harry Bamford Memorial match ticket, 8 May 1959. A combined Bristol XI played Arsenal before 28,347 spectators, who paid their respects to one of football's gentlemen.

Bristol Rovers, 1959/60 season. From left to right, back row: Ray Mabbutt, Norman Sykes, Malcolm Norman, David Pyle, Doug Hillard, Josser Watling. Front row: Granville Smith, Alfie Biggs, Geoff Bradford, Dai Ward, Peter Hooper.

The introduction of floodlights ensured evening matches could be arranged to kick-off at 7.30pm. They were used for the first time for the visit of Ipswich Town on 6 September 1959.

Enjoying a well-deserved, end-of-match cuppa, c. 1959. David Pyle, Norman Sykes, 'Josser' Watling and Geoff Bradford relax after another tiring performance in the Eastville mud.

F.A. CUP—4th Round   KICK-OFF 3.0 p.m.

BRISTOL ROVERS v. PRESTON NORTH END

R.   BRISTOL ROVERS   L.
Colours—Blue and White Quarters, White Shorts

NORMAN

HILLARD (2)   WATLING (Captain) (3)

SYKES (4)   FROWEN (5)   MABBUTT (6)

PETHERBRIDGE (7) BIGGS (8) BRADFORD (9) WARD (10) HOOPER (11)

Referee :   Linesmen :
Mr. J. K. TAYLOR (Wolverhampton)   Mr. F. G. ALFORD (Red Flag)
                                        Mr. W. H. J. COLE (Yellow Flag)

TAYLOR (11)   SNEDDON (10)   FINNEY (9)   THOMPSON (8)   MAYERS (7)

SMITH (6)   DUNN (5)   MILNE (4)

WALTON (3)   WILSON (2)

ELSE

L.   PRESTON NORTH END   R.

THIS GAME RELAYED TO 22 HOSPITALS BY "HOSPITALS BROADCASTS"

Home or Away ... team up with

Easier on the feet!
Warmer too!

ARIES

WASHABLE INNER SOCKS
From most Shoe Stores

Bristol Rovers *v.* Preston North End programme from the match held on 30 January 1960. This FA Cup fourth round tie, which ended 3-3, attracted the largest ever attendance at Eastville, with 38,472 watching the match.

Bristol Rovers, 1960/61 season. From left to right, back row: Sampson, Hillard, Pyle, Norman, Frowen, Mabbutt. Front row: Petherbridge, Biggs, Purdon, Ward, Hooper.

Five

Relegation and Back to the Third Division
The 1960s

BRISTOL ROVERS 4,   LEEDS UNITED 4

LAST MONDAY — GEORGE PETHERBRIDGE STARTS IT ALL OFF!

Bristol Rovers 4 Leeds United 4. This match took place on 29 August 1960 and was one of the most remarkable comebacks in the club's history. Leeds were winning 4-0 at half-time but second half goals from George Petherbridge (pictured), Ian Hamilton and a pair from Peter Hooper entertained a crowd of 19,028 supporters.

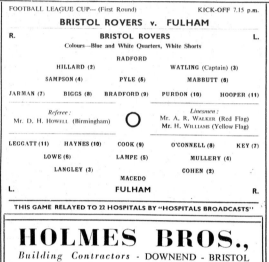

FOOTBALL LEAGUE CUP— (First Round)   KICK-OFF 7.15 p.m.

BRISTOL ROVERS v. FULHAM

R.   **BRISTOL ROVERS**   L.
Colours—Blue and White Quarters, White Shorts

RADFORD

HILLARD (2)   WATLING (Captain) (3)

SAMPSON (4)   PYLE (5)   MABBUTT (6)

JARMAN (7)   BIGGS (8)   BRADFORD (9)   PURDON (10)   HOOPER (11)

Referee :   *Linesmen :*
Mr. D. H. HOWELL (Birmingham)   O   Mr. A. R. WALKER (Red Flag)
Mr. H. WILLIAMS (Yellow Flag)

LEGGATT (11)   HAYNES (10)   COOK (9)   O'CONNELL (8)   KEY (7)

LOWE (6)   LAMPE (5)   MULLERY (4)

LANGLEY (3)   COHEN (2)

MACEDO

L.   **FULHAM**   R.

THIS GAME RELAYED TO 22 HOSPITALS BY "HOSPITALS BROADCASTS"

Rovers *v.* Fulham programme for the first ever League Cup tie, held on 26 September 1960. Rovers kicked off at 7.15pm, whilst all the other ties that evening started fifteen minutes later.

Harold Jarman (out of photograph) is credited with the club's first ever goal in the League Cup competition, scored during the 2-1 victory over Fulham.

Liverpool scoring against Rovers at Eastville on the opening day of the season, 19 August 1961. It was the first of seven consecutive defeats Rovers suffered and contributed to an unenviable club record.

This goal by Luton Town at Kenilworth Road, on 28 April 1962, resulted in relegation for Rovers after nine seasons in Division Two.

Bristol Rovers, 1962/63 season. From left to right, back row: Ryden, Gardner, Stone, Hendy, Hillard, Baker. Middle row: Bradford, Bumpstead, Sykes, Million, Hall, Humes, Frowen, Jones G. Front row: Slocombe, Oldfield, Jones K., Mabbutt, Hamilton, Williams K., Jarman, Jones R., Davis.

MILLION'S MISTAKES

So solid Rovers

Draw at Bradford —despite errors

by ROBIN PERRY

BRADFORD 2, BRISTOL ROVERS 2.

Bristol Rovers gained a valuable point at Bradford this afternoon after twice losing the lead.

It was a nightmare game for goalkeeper Ex. Million. He was at fault in the two Bradford goals, jointly sharing the responsibility of the first blunder with Ray Mabbutt.

The second goal should have been comfortably cleared but he completely missed the ball to give Hector a simple opportunity.

Rovers ease their worries

Bradford 2 Bristol Rovers 2

Bristol Rovers upset Bradford's hopes of easing their relegation worries by twice taking the lead and defending stubbornly that on to keep a point, which could help their own bottom-of-the-table troubles.

Newspaper match reports from the Bradford Park Avenue v. Rovers match on 20 April 1963. A tense relegation match for both clubs ended all square at 2-2. Rovers came from behind twice, after goals were gifted to the opposition by Million, the goalkeeper. The significance of this did not become apparent for another week.

Green 'Un headlines reveal the bribery scandal involving Rovers goalkeeper Es Million and centre forward Keith Williams. Both players were suspended by the club and, subsequently, found guilty and banned from professional football.

The winter of 1962 saw hundreds of League matches postponed. Rovers did not play at all between 15 December and 9 February. This photograph from an end of season match, played on 11 May 1963, shows Geoff Bradford taking on the Wrexham defence.

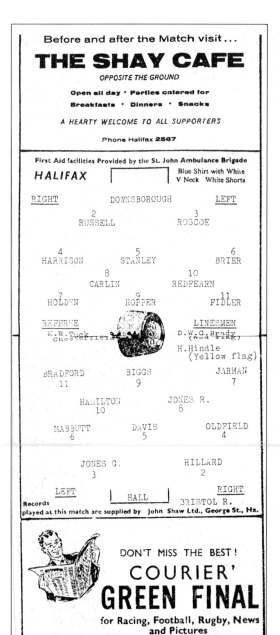

First Aid facilities Provided by the St. John Ambulance Brigade

HALIFAX Blue Shirt with White
V Neck White Shorts

RIGHT DOWNSBOROUGH LEFT

2
RUSSELL

3
ROSCOE

4
HARRISON

5
STANLEY

6
BRIER

8
CARLIN

10
REDFEARN

7
HOLDEN

9
HOPPER

11
FIDLER

REFEREE
K.R.Tuck
Chesterfield

LINESMEN
D.W.G.Brady
(Red flag)

H.Hindle
(Yellow flag)

BRADFORD
11

BIGGS
9

JARMAN
7

HAMILTON
10

JONES R.
8

MABBUTT
6

DAVIS
5

OLDFIELD
4

JONES G.
3

HILLARD
2

LEFT HALL RIGHT
BRISTOL R.

Records
played at this match are supplied by John Shaw Ltd., George St., Hx.

BRISTOL EVENING POST →

Hamilton's two goals put paid to Halifax

Halifax Town 2, Bristol Rovers 3

Bristol Rovers escaped relegation to the Fourth Division on Saturday by beating bottom-of-the-table Halifax Town 3—2 on a rain-soaked pitch at The Shay.

Over 500 fans travelled up from Bristol to cheer on Rovers last ditch fight for Third Division survival, and they played a key roll in this all important success.

They left Halifax in a jubilant mood, but not until they had experienced a thoroughly nerve racking second half.

An urgent, forceful Rovers team skated over the slippery surface to snatch a second-minute lead, when Bobbie Jones's shot was deflected on to the post and over the line

Ten minutes later, they were two goals up. Geoff Bradford brilliantly beat Russell on the bye line, thumped over a centre, and Ian Hamilton moved in to leave Downsborough helpless with a strong, close range header.

It looked as if Rovers' relegation worries were all over. Halifax looked an untidy, dispirited team, not capable of the fight or the method needed to break Rovers' early grip.

Rovers almost paid the penalty for not consolidating their advantage, but they deserved victory.

Halifax Town: Downsborough, Russell, Roscoe, Harrison, Stanley, Brier; Priestley, Carlin, Hopper, Holden, Fidler.

Bristol Rovers: Hall, Hillard, Jones (G); Oldfield, Davis, Mabbutt; Jarman, Jones (R), Biggs, Hamilton, Bradford

Not enough

One more Rovers' goal would have left the result in no doubt at all. But good saves by Downsborough from Jarman and Bradford, and a miss by Bobbie Jones restricted Rovers to a two-goal interval lead.

It soon became apparent that this was not going to be enough. Halifax reappeared a transformed side. Hopper and Fidler brought smart saves from Bernard Hall, and a last second headed clearance by Mabbutt robbed Holden of an easy chance.

When the home team scored in the 56th minute it was no more than their spirited revival had deserved. Hall went out for Fidler's and Paddy Stanley, Halifax's big centre-half, crashed a superb header into the back of the net.

Tension returned to Rovers' play. Bradford missed an easy chance of restoring the two goals lead, but Halifax, sensing a chance of relieving some of their relegation blues, remained lively, and after 69 minutes scored an equaliser.

Bill Holden broke away down the right, squared a pass over to Fidler, and the left winger beat Hall with a smart drive from a narrow angle.

Vital goal

For a few minutes, Rovers and their fans were despondent, but the Eastville team were soon urged on to fresh efforts, and the goal that kept them in the Third Division was not far away.

Bobby Jones's in-swinging corner from the left gave Hamilton a chance to head his second goal in the 74th minute. Rovers fans could breath again.

Left: Halifax v. Rovers programme for the fixture played on 18 May 1963. This was a vital match that Rovers had to win to ensure they were not relegated to Division Four. Right: Match reports from that important game at Halifax

Harold Jarman was a popular Bristol-born winger who scored many memorable goals for Rovers in a career which lasted fourteen seasons. Jarman scored 127 goals in 442 League appearances. He had a brief spell as caretaker manager in December 1980 and helped Rovers avoid relegation. Jarman has enjoyed many years as the youth team coach and has been responsible for grooming many young players who have made it into the first team.

Bristol Rovers F.C.

Bristol Rovers, 1964/65 season. From left to right, back row: Oldfield, Hillard, Hall, Jones G., Stone. Front row: Jarman, Brown, Jones R., Davis, Hamilton, Munro.

Rovers' cinder training pitch was used as a car park during match days. This photograph was taken from the Eastville floodlights by Ernie Clark, the stadium electrician, in around 1966.

Aerial view overlooking Eastville Stadium's south stand and enclosure, *c.* 1966.

Eastville Stadium taken from the Muller Road terracing, *c.* 1966.

Rovers enjoyed a good season in 1966/67, but missed out on promotion after a slump in form. They only won twice in their final thirteen matches and finished fifth. From left to right, back row: Petts, Munro, Parsons, Hillard, Briggs, Hall, Taylor, Ronaldson, Stone, Mabbutt. Front row: Jarman, Frude, Brown, Davis, Biggs, Hamilton, Jones R.

Rovers enjoyed an exciting FA Cup run in the 1968/69 season. After winning at Bolton they were drawn at Everton, who were to become League Champions. Rovers were narrowly beaten 1-0 in front of over 55,000 spectators. The squad consisted of, from left to right, back row: Munro, Taylor S., Lowrie, Roberts, White, Taylor L., Parsons, Prince, Lloyd, Stanton. Middle row: Jarman, Williams R., Gadston, Plumb, Ronaldson, Graydon, Jones R. Front row: Mabbutt, Brown, Barney, Jones W., Petts, Higgins.

Six

Promotion and the 'Smash and Grab' Era

The 1970s

BRISTOL ROVERS FOOTBALL CLUB Ltd.

No 12141

Bristol Rovers v. Aston Villa

F.L. CUP — 5th ROUND

Tuesday, 17th Nov., 1970.   Kick-off 7.30 p.m.

Ground 6/-

General Manager/Secretary

To be given up at Ground Turnstiles.

STAPLETON RD. or MULLER RD. ENTRANCES.

IN THE EVENT OF POSTPONEMENT THIS TICKET WILL BE AVAILABLE FOR THE RE-ARRANGED FIXTURE — NO MONEY WILL BE REFUNDED.

Young, Humphrys & Lodge, Ltd., Bristol.

A ticket for Rovers' fifth round League Cup tie, on 17 November 1970, which ended in a 1-1 draw at Eastville. Villa won the replay with a last minute goal and, subsequently, went through to the final.

BRISTOL ROVERS, 1970-71 . . . Left to right—
back row: Wayne Jones, Lindsay Parsons, Frankie
Prince, Dick Sheppard, Stuart Taylor, Phil Roberts,
Don Megson (player-coach). Front row: Ray
Graydon, Bobby Jones, Robin Stubbs, Bryn Jones,

Bristol Rovers, 1970/71 season. From left to right, back row: Jones W., Parsons, Prince,
Sheppard, Taylor, Roberts, Megson. Front row: Graydon, Jones R., Stubbs, Jones B., Jarman,
Gilbert.

Rovers' goalkeeper Dick Sheppard pulls off the match-winning save from Sheffield United's
Ted Hemsley (in the penalty shoot-out) to win the Watney Cup on 5 August 1972.

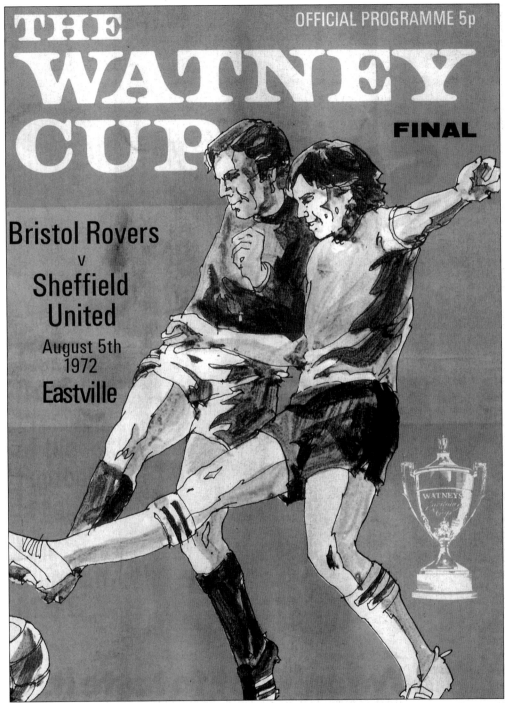

OFFICIAL PROGRAMME 5p

THE WATNEY CUP FINAL

Bristol Rovers
v
Sheffield United
August 5th
1972
Eastville

Programme for the Watney Cup final. As holders, Rovers automatically entered the 1973 competition, but were beaten by Hull City in the first round.

LEAGUE CUP
THIRD ROUND
REPLAY

Wednesday October 11th 1972
Kick Off 7-30 p.m.

No. 10
5p

MANCHESTER
UNITED

VERSUS

BRISTOL
ROVERS

THE OFFICIAL PROGRAMME OF MANCHESTER UNITED FOOTBALL CLUB LIMITED

On 11 October 1972, Rovers beat Manchester United 2-1 in a replay after a 1-1 draw at Eastville, with Dick Sheppard saving a George Best penalty.

Rovers reverted back to the blue and white quarters in 1973/74. They proved successful, as Rovers gained promotion in that season. From left to right, back row: Sheppard, Eadie, Crabtree. Middle row: Parsons, Prince, Green, Warboys, Taylor, Rudge, Bannister, John. Front row: Dobson, Fearnley, Aitken, Jacobs, Stephens, Jones B., Stanton.

SATURDAY 1st DECEMBER 1973

BRIGHTON & HOVE

ALBION

v

BRISTOL ROVERS
DIVISION III

7p OFFICIAL PROGRAMME
WITH 'LEAGUE FOOTBALL'

A programme for Rovers' (club record) 8-2 defeat of Brian Clough's Brighton on 1 December 1973. The match was featured on national television and underlined Rovers' status as a talented Division Three team.

After their goalscoring exploits at Brighton, where Bruce Bannister (left) scored three and Alan Warboys netted four, the duo became known as 'Smash and Grab'. Warboys was Rovers' top goalscorer, with twenty-two goals, while Bannister finished with eighteen.

Bruce Bannister takes on the Nottingham Forest defence in a thrilling third round FA Cup tie. This took place on 6 January 1974, which was Rovers' first ever Sunday match. Rovers were beaten 4-3 by their Division One opponents.

Alan Warboys, a £35,000 signing from Cardiff City in March 1973, proved to be a valuable acquisition. He accumulated fifty-three goals in 141 League appearances before being sold to Fulham, for £30,000, in February 1977.

Rovers' supporters celebrate promotion back to Division Two on 27 April 1974, after an absence of twelve years, following the final home game of the season against Brighton.

Bristol Rovers, 1977/78 season. From left to right, back row: Parsons, Bater, Jones G., Thomas, Stephens, Jones V. Middle row: Aitken, White, Taylor, Harding, Pulis, Britten. Front row: Foreman, Staniforth, Prince, Hamilton, Evans, Powell.

Bobby Gould made a remarkable League debut for Rovers on 15 October 1977. Here he is scoring one of a splendid hat-trick of goals against Blackburn Rovers, in a 4-1 victory at Eastville. Gould had two separate spells as manager of Rovers during the 1980s.

At 6' 5", Stuart Taylor was the club's tallest ever player. Described as a gentle giant, he was a permanent fixture in Rovers' defence from 1965 until 1980. A model of consistency, Taylor amassed a formidable club record 546 League appearances, which is unlikely ever be bettered. Taylor was also a regular goalscorer from corners and scored twenty-eight times during his one-club career.

Paul Randall attracted a lot of attention after the nineteen-year-old scored two superb goals to knock Division One Southampton out of the FA Cup on 28 January 1978. The match, at Eastville, was watched by over 26,000 supporters.

One of the most exciting matches ever seen at Eastville was the 5-5 draw with Charlton Athletic on 18 November 1978. David Williams, who scored two goals that day, takes on the Londoners' defence. Paul Randall scored a hat-trick. Remarkably, ten goals had been scored in the first seventy minutes, but none were added in the remainder of the match.

Stewart Barrowclough became Rovers' record signing when he joined them from Birmingham City for £100,000. The former England under-23 winger enjoyed some very good performances and was particularly accurate from the penalty spot.

Bristol Rovers, 1979/80 season. From left to right, back row: Penny, Jones V., England, Harding, Palmer, Griffiths, Brown. Middle row: Bater, Hughes, Pulis, Thomas, Kite, Stevens, Williams G., Dean, Mabbutt. Front row: Emmanuel, Gillies, Barrowclough, Cooper (Manager), Bates, Barrett, Williams D..

A fire on the morning of Sunday 17 August 1980 devastated Rovers' old wooden South Stand. Besides the loss of income from the seating, the club's dressing rooms were also gone, which meant that Rovers had to temporarily share Ashton Gate to ensure the continuation of League fixtures.

Bob Lee, a £50,000 signing, challenges Newcastle United goalkeeper Hardwick in a game, which ended goal-less, on 27 September 1980. This was one of five games to be played at Ashton Gate following the fire.

Mike Barrett, a skilful winger, is being congratulated after scoring his first League goal in a 3-3 draw with Sheffield Wednesday on 18 October 1980. Sadly, Barrett died of cancer in August 1984 at the age of twenty-three. Barrett made 129 League appearances, scoring eighteen goals.

Southampton's Charlie George is denied by Rovers' goalkeeper, Phil Kite, in a fourth round FA Cup tie at The Dell on 24 January 1981. The cup-tie, won 3-1 by the Saints, was a welcome break from the League programme as Rovers struggled to score goals. They were relegated just five months later.

Alan Ball, an England international and World Cup winner in 1966, had a five month spell with Rovers in 1983. He scored this, his first goal, in a 2-0 win over Plymouth Argyle at Eastville on 5 February 1983.

Rovers celebrated their centenary in August 1983 by playing their first ever opponents, Wotton, wearing a specially-made black strip with a yellow sash (these were the colours used by the Black Arabs – Rovers' original name some 100 years before).

Young full-back Neil Slatter won ten Welsh caps while he was with Rovers. He is included in this team group for the 1984/85 season. From left to right, back row: Kendall (Kit Man), Dolling (Trainer), White, Bannon, Cashley, Kite, Parkin, McCaffery, Williams G., Jarman (Coach), Jones (Assistant Manager). Front row: Bater, Slatter, Williams B., Williams D. (Player/manager), Holloway, Stephens, Randall.

A victory at Ashton Gate over rivals Bristol City is always sweet. This goal, by Paul Randall, set up an unexpected 3-1 win in a second round FA Cup tie on 8 December 1984.

Brian Williams, a left-winger or left-back, was a very reliable penalty taker. This successful spot-kick – his second of the match – came in the 3-0 defeat of Brentford on 6 April 1985.

Trevor Morgan scores against Division One Leicester City to help knock them out of the FA Cup on 4 January 1986. It was the first time Rovers had knocked out a team of that stature for almost twenty-eight years.

Former England midfielder Gerry Francis appeared in thirty-two League games for Rovers, adding valuable experience to a young team. He returned as manager in July 1987. The squad for the 1985/86 season was, from left to right, back row: Weston, O'Connor, Bater, White, Randall, Mehew, Howells, Obi. Middle row: Jarman, Badock, Spring, Parkin, Green, Carter, Tanner, Scales, Kendall (Kit Man). Front row: Penrice, Jones, Bradshaw (Director), Bennett (Chief Executive), Gould (Manager), Flook (Director), Davies, Cockram.

As a 'thank you' to the fans, the Rovers directors generously paid for their travel to Walsall on 18 March 1986. Unfortunately, the players let them down with a 6-0 defeat at Fellows Park. Manager Bobby Gould leaves the pitch a very angry man after the game.

Rovers finally left Eastville, their historic home for ninety years, on 26 April 1986, following this 1-1 draw with Chesterfield. The move to ground-share Bath City's Twerton Park was the only viable option. Rovers received financial compensation of £280,000 from the Bristol Stadium Company for giving up their tenant's rights.

Rovers supporters invade the pitch at the final whistle after the Chesterfield game.

Seven

The Decade At
Twerton Park
1986-96

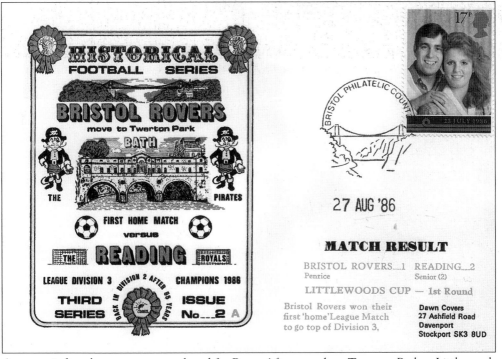

A souvenir first day cover was produced for Rovers' first match at Twerton Park, a Littlewoods Cup tie with Reading on 27 August 1986. During their first season in Bath there were problems with the playing surface and many matches were postponed.

Rovers struggled in their first season at Bath. They had to win their final match of the season at Newport County, on 9 May 1987, to ensure they were not relegated to Division Four for the first time in their history. Phil Purnell proved to be the match-winner with this goal in a 1-0 victory.

Nigel Martyn pulls off a penalty save from Bristol City's Rob Newman on 25 March 1989. Cornish-born Martyn proved to be a very valuable asset – after completing 101 League appearances for Rovers, Martyn became Britain's first £1 million goalkeeper on his transfer to Crystal Palace in November 1989.

Eight

Wembley and the
Play-offs
The 1990s

Gary Penrice scores the only goal of the Division Three Play-off semi-final first-leg defeat of Fulham on 21 May 1989. In the second leg, Rovers won 4-0. Penrice was sold for £500,000 in November 1989, but returned for a second spell in July 1997.

The two play-off matches against Port Vale finished 1-1 at Twerton and 1-0 to the home side at Vale Park on 3 June 1989.

David Mehew enjoyed a magnificent season as Rovers won the Division Three championship. Mehew finished as the club's top scorer, with eighteen goals. Remarkably, many of his goals, like the one featured here at Reading on 6 March 1990, were match-winners.

This was the goal which ensured Rovers reached Wembley for the first time in their history: David Mehew heads the only goal in the first leg of the Leyland Daf Southern final against Notts County on 28 March 1990.

A goal-less draw in the second leg at Notts County – which was a very tense match for both Rovers players and their supporters – ended with happy scenes of celebration long into the night on 26 April 1990.

Ian Holloway scores in the most important Bristol derby ever, on 2 May 1990. His goal, from the penalty spot, was Rovers' third and it ensured promotion to Division Two. Four days later, another 3-0 victory at Blackpool ensured the championship. Holloway has enjoyed three spells

as a player and, more recently, as manager of Rovers in a career which has seen him proudly appear in over 400 matches for the club.

Devon White scores Rovers' equaliser against Tranmere Rovers at Wembley in the Leyland Daf Trophy final, but the Birkenhead side managed a second goal to record a 2-1 win. The 33,000

Rovers fans certainly enjoyed their day at the 'Twin Towers'.

Manager Gerry Francis was an enormous influence in turning Rovers into a solid team. His work on the training ground changed the side into a formidable unit. Here he is, pictured in the coach on its way to Wembley, on 20 May 1990.

A programme for the final. The match attracted a crowd of 48,402.

Captain Vaughan Jones holds aloft the Division Three Championship Trophy, before his testimonial match against a Gerry Francis XI. Jones enjoyed two spells with Rovers, appearing in almost 400 League games in fifteen seasons.

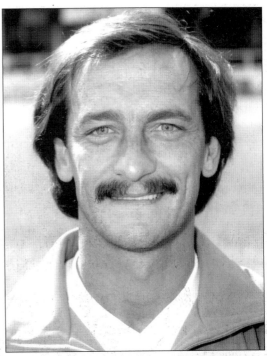

Kenny Hibbit Assistant Manager to
Gerry Francis, Hibbits coaching skills
contributed to Rovers promotion.

Rovers players celebrate the Division Three Championship and a remarkable record of just five
defeats in forty-six League matches – a club record. From left to right, back row: McClean,
White, Reece, Nixon. Middle row: Mehew, Saunders, Alexander, Hazel, Willmott, Browning,
Kelly, Yates. Front row: Bloomer, Jones, Purnell, Twentyman, Holloway, Parkin.

An arson attack on the Grandstand in October 1990 caused further financial problems at Twerton Park, with the club having to rent temporary seating.

Ian Holloway has enjoyed three spells at Rovers, making his debut in 1981 before moving onto Wimbledon, and Brentford. From 1987 to 1991 he was a member of Rovers championship team, before a move to QPR. An offer in 1996 to manage his home town club ensured his return.

Rovers players Geoff Twentyman, Steve Yates, Justin Skinner and Marcus Browning salute the travelling Gasheads, following the remarkable 5-4 aggregate League Cup victory over Bristol City at Ashton Gate, 9 October 1991. Twentyman spent a year as assistant manager under Holloway in 1996.

Rovers enjoyed an exciting FA Cup experience with Liverpool on 5 February 1992. Carl Saunders scored this memorable goal at Twerton Park, past Bruce Grobbelaar, and the game finished as a 1-1 draw. The crowd of 9,464 realised record receipts of £62,480.

In the replay at Anfield, on 11 February 1992, over 5,000 travelling fans saw a superb opening goal, a volley by Carl Saunders. But Liverpool, with goals from Steve McManaman and Dean Saunders, won 2-1.

An aerial photograph of Twerton Park, Rovers' temporary home for a decade.

Aerial photograph of Eastville Stadium, after Rovers left for the last time.

The 'Golden Goal' – Paul Miller scores Rovers' equaliser in extra-time at Crewe Alexandra, on 17 May 1995, to ensure a place (on the away goals rule) in the play-off final at Wembley.

Rovers' top goalscorer Marcus Stewart, with twenty-one goals, is congratulated by excited Rovers fans at the final whistle at Crewe.

Rovers supporters at Wembley for the Play Off Final.

Justin Skinner is denied a goal at Wembley in the Play Off Final against Huddersfield Town.

Division Two Play-off final programme

This equalising goal by Marcus Stewart in the final against Huddersfield Town on 28 May 1995 could not be added to, which meant a second defeat at Wembley. The 2-1 loss was a major disappointment for both the Rovers players and supporters.

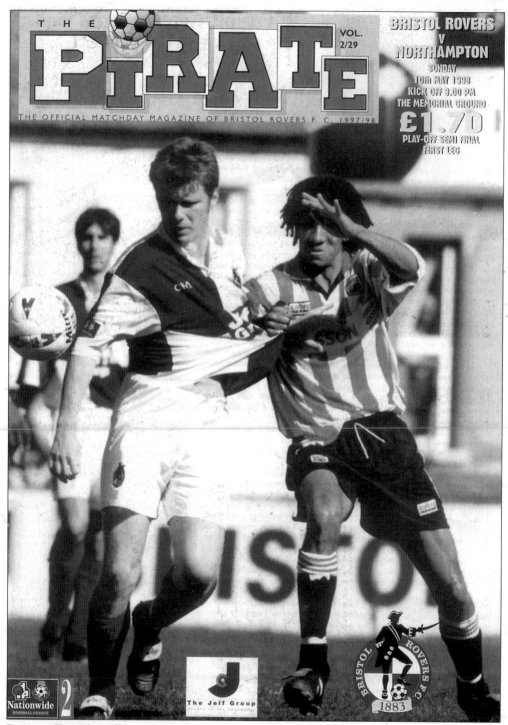

Division Two Play-off semi-final programme. Northampton were soundly beaten 3-1 in a match which realised record match receipts of £74,952. However, Rovers were soundly defeated 3-0 in the second leg in an emotional night at the Sixfields Stadium. Rovers matchday programme won the Programme of the Year award in 1998.

Memorial move – The Centenary Grandstand at the Memorial Stadium. When the West Grandstand was completed, in October 1996, it improved the facilities with executive boxes, new dressing rooms and extra seating. The overall capacity at the stadium rose to 9,173.

A home of our own at last! The Memorial Stadium becomes Rovers' first 'home' of their own for over fifty-eight years, after its purchase from Bristol Rugby Club, for £2.3million. Rovers directors Barry Bradshaw, Geoff Dunford, Ron Craig, Vernon Stokes and Denis Dunford and their families celebrate this tremendous acquisition.

Barry Hayles was a very talented goalscorer, who joined Rovers from Stevenage for £200,000. In less than eighteen months, Hayles had scored thirty-two goals in sixty-two League appearances, and was sold to Fulham for £2 million in November 1998.